God Bless America

PRAYERS FOR OUR COUNTRY

Manufactured in U.S.A.

9 8 7 6 5 4 3 2 1

ISBN:0-7853-6658-X

 Publications International, Ltd.

The Spirit of America

On the morning of September 11, 2001, the very fabric of our nation was torn apart. Terrorists attacked New York's World Trade Center and the Pentagon in Washington, D.C., leaving thousands dead and wounded and an entire country emotionally devastated. Americans watched and listened in horror as the tragedy unfolded on their televisions and radios. What had started out as just another Tuesday turned into a day no one would ever forget, a time of darkness and grief that few citizens had ever experienced before.

When tragedy and loss of unimaginable proportion struck our shores, our very humanity trembled at its core. People lost faith in what was good and right in their world. They became angry, afraid, and untrusting of others. They questioned their freedom and security in an ever-changing world. They tried to make sense of that which was senseless.

But out of the ashes of their suffering, Americans rose like the glorious phoenix. With heads held high and proud, Americans everywhere opened their arms and their hearts and jumped to the ready to help their fellow citizens in need. Neighbors reached out to neighbors. Strangers became friends.

All over this great land, people responded with an unprecedented outpouring of support, prayers, money, and donations of blood. Hundreds flocked to the crisis sites to offer their assistance. Doctors, nurses, police, and firefighters went beyond the call of duty and became heroes, risking their own lives for those who might still be alive in the debris. Average citizens dug deep into their hearts and pocketbooks, giving to a vast array of charities that supported the victims.

September 11, and the days that followed, proved one thing: The American spirit cannot be crippled. Not by disasters or acts of violence. Not by anger or fear or ignorance. For what makes America so strong is the quality and character of its people and their ability to find good amidst the darkest evil—to find hope where others see only the rubble of devastation.

All Americans cope with the tragedy of September 11, no matter how far they live from the sites. And support for our government and military runs high in the face of such evil. Good *will* prevail.

May the prayers, poems, songs, and reflections in this publication remind you of what it truly means to be an American. May you and your loved ones find comfort, strength, courage, inspiration, and wisdom in the following pages. May each word fill you with hope and gratitude for our nation and for the future of our children. And may you be reminded of all the wonderful things in your own lives, things you might have taken for granted until now.

God bless America, land that we love. Land of courage, compassion, and freedom. From sea to shining sea....

To Be an American

What does it mean to be an American? If you ask any of the more than 280 million citizens of the United States, chances are you will get more than 280 million unique answers. But they all will have one common thread running through them— that to be an American is to be free.

Which leads to the question, what is freedom? Most Americans will say that freedom is the opportunity to make choices based upon their values, goals, and desires. Some might say it's the chance to be whoever they want to be. Still others might suggest it is the ability to speak their mind without worry of retribution. Freedom means many things to many people, yet we often neglect to think about what it means to us until there is a threat of it being taken away.

Terrorist actions, war, martial law—these things run rampant in many troubled nations, yet America has had very little experience with challenges to the day-to-day freedoms we exercise without a second thought.

Think about how blessed we are as a nation, as a people, to be free. Free to think, act, speak, and dream with no limitations to what we can accomplish. But in order to keep the freedoms we hold so dear, we must never take them for granted. Honoring and fighting for freedom both here and the world over— *that* is what it means to be an American.

With the supporting hands of friends and helpers, we feel God's strong grasp and hold on, no longer alone.

Be angry but do not sin; do not let the sun go down on your anger.

Ephesians 4:26

Beyond the Call of Duty

*T*hey are faceless, nameless strangers. They are men and women who few Americans see or think about or talk about until we need them. They are nurses, doctors, firefighters, and police officers. They are Red Cross volunteers and rescue teams sent into the line of battle to do what they can to save lives.

During our nation's most trying times, we have watched in awe as average, everyday people transformed into real-life heroes simply because they were doing their job. Men and women

who endangered their own personal safety to enter burning buildings; nurses and doctors working around the clock to tend to the wounded; relief workers traveling across the country to help their fellow citizens in another state; police officers putting their own bodies in the line of fire to protect civilians.

In a nation that so often reserves its hero worship for celebrities and athletes, disasters remind us of the real heroes, the real shining stars going beyond the call of duty to serve and to protect, even when their own lives are at risk.

They are angels in uniform.

I wait for the Lord, my soul waits, and in his word I hope.

Psalm 130:5

*F*aith is a true sign of bravery. It is looking forward to the future despite challenges and adversity; it is trusting in something that you can neither see nor touch yet knowing it is always there guiding you along life's path.

Guide Us

*H*elp us, Lord! Everything seems to be spinning out of control, and there's no help in sight but you. Gratefully, we know that putting our trust in you is the most productive thing we can do. For when we aren't in control anymore, you still are. We place all that's happening right now in your hands and ask that you help us sort out solutions to these problems we face. For we know that with you all things are possible.

*P*erseverance will accomplish all things.

American proverb

*L*ord, heal the differences between our nation and those who hate us. Amen.

I long for reconciliation and peace, but I don't know how to make it happen. Help me to do my part. Show me how to walk in your way of peace, God, and let that peace permeate each person I meet.

The Star-Spangled Banner

O say, can you see, by the dawn's early light,
What so proudly we hail'd at the twilight's last gleaming?
Whose broad stripes and bright stars, thro' the perilous fight,
O'er the ramparts we watch'd, were so gallantly streaming?
And the rockets' red glare,
  the bombs bursting in air,
Gave proof thro' the night
  that our flag was still there.
O say does that star-spangled
  banner yet wave
O'er the land of the free and
  the home of the brave?

Francis Scott Key, 1814

*E*ach one of us needs to look after the good of the people around us, asking ourselves, "How can I help?" That's exactly what Jesus did. He didn't make it easy for himself by avoiding people's troubles, but waded right in and helped out. "I took on the troubles of the world" is the way Scripture puts it.

Romans 15:2–3, The Message

Freedoms

God, my freedoms are much like the air I breathe; they are taken for granted until they are taken away. So today I want to pause a minute and thank you for the freedoms of all kinds that I have been able to enjoy.

These blessings include choosing what I will wear, being able to freely worship, voting for whomever I wish, deciding whether and whom I will marry, and having the freedom to travel from place to place.

These are just a few items on a very long list. God, you are the author of freedom, the champion of the privilege of making one's own choices. Help me to honor you today by choosing well and wisely.

*I*ncline your ear to me; rescue me speedily. Be a rock of refuge for me, a strong fortress to save me.

Psalm 31:2

*M*y heart is broken, Lord, but I know you can fix it. As I learn to depend on you, give me the same thing you gave your servant David: strength and a song.

Battle Hymn of the Republic

Mine eyes have seen the glory of the coming of the Lord;
He is trampling out the vintage where the grapes
   of wrath are stored;
He hath loosed the fateful lightning of His
   terrible swift sword,
His truth is marching on.

Chorus
Glory! Glory! Hallelujah!
Glory! Glory! Hallelujah!
Glory! Glory! Hallelujah!
His truth is marching on.

I have seen Him in the watch-fires of a
   hundred circling camps;
They have builded Him an altar in the
   evening dews and damps;
I can read His righteous sentence by the dim
   and flaring lamps,
His days are marching on.

Chorus

I have read a fiery gospel, writ in burnished rows of steel;
As ye deal with My contemners, so with you
   My grace shall deal;
Let the Hero born of woman, crush the serpent with His heel,
Since God is marching on.

Chorus

He has sounded forth the trumpet that shall never call retreat;
He is sifting out the hearts of men before His judgement seat;
O, be swift, my soul, to answer Him! be jubilant my feet!
Our God is marching on.

Chorus

In the beauty of the lilies Christ was born across the sea,
With a glory in His bosom that transfigures you and me;
As He died to make men holy, let us die to make men free,
While God is marching on.

Julia Ward Howe, 1861

Praise be to the God and Father of our Lord Jesus Christ, the Father of compassion and the God of all comfort, who comforts us in all our troubles, so that we can comfort those in any trouble with the comfort we ourselves have received from God.

2 Corinthians 1:3–4 NIV

When I die I desire no better winding sheet than the Stars and Stripes, and no softer pillow than the Constitution of my country.

Andrew Johnson

A Prayer for Healing

God, hear our prayers. When we are afraid, give us courage to face our fears. When we are angry, fill our hearts with your precious peace. When we want to hate, teach us to love instead. When we want to avenge, teach us instead to forgive. When we are sick, heal us with your comforting balm. When we are hurt, bind up our wounds and make us whole again.

Hear our prayers for healing, for mercy, for love. Let us not be tempted to turn to darkness, or to give in to fear, but instead fortify us against evil and make smooth the path before us so that we shall not stumble.

Amen.

Don't fret or worry. Instead of worrying, pray. Let petitions and praises shape your worries into prayers, letting God know your concerns. Before you know it, a sense of God's wholeness, everything coming together for good, will come and settle you down. It's wonderful what happens when Christ displaces worry at the center of your life.

Philippians 4:6–7

*F*rom each of life's misfortunes, large or small, comes a new beginning, an opportunity to renew your faith in the future.

*E*ach prayer is a message of faith in God. We are saying, "I trust you; lead me. I believe in you; guide me. I need you; show me." When we offer ourselves openly, he will always answer.

Americans by Choice

We have gathered here to affirm a faith, a faith in a common purpose, a common conviction, a common devotion. Some of us have chosen America as the land of our adoption; the rest have come from those who did the same. For this reason we have some right to consider ourselves a picked group, a group of those who had the courage to break from the past and brave the dangers and the loneliness of a strange land. What was the object that nerved us, or those who went before us, to this

choice? We sought liberty: freedom from oppression, freedom from want, freedom to be ourselves.

Judge Learned Hand, from a speech in New York during
"I Am an American Day" festivities on May 21, 1944

He has sent me to bind up the brokenhearted,

to proclaim freedom for the captives

and release from darkness for the prisoners,

to proclaim the year of the Lord's favor

and the day of vengeance of our God,

to comfort all who mourn,

and provide for those who grieve in Zion—

to bestow on them a crown of beauty

instead of ashes,

the oil of gladness

instead of mourning,

and a garment of praise

instead of a spirit of despair.

Isaiah 61:1–3a NIV

Be strong and courageous; do not be frightened or dismayed, for the Lord your God is with you wherever you go.

Joshua 1:9

Hopeful eyes look upward, penetrating the thick blanket of clouds to the clear blue skies beyond.

God Makes a Path

God makes a path, provides a guide,
     And feeds a wilderness;
His glorious name, while breath remains,
     O that I may confess.

Lost many a time, I have had no guide,
     No house but a hollow tree!
In stormy winter night no fire,
     No food, no company;

In Him I found a house, a bed,
     A table, company;
No cup so bitter but's made sweet,
     Where God shall sweetening be.

Clergyman and Rhode Island founder Roger Williams (1603–1683)

For I am convinced that neither death, nor life, nor angels, nor rulers, nor things present, nor things to come, nor powers, nor height, nor depth, nor anything else in all creation, will be able to separate us from the love of God in Christ Jesus our Lord.

Romans 8:38–39

What Do We Tell Our Children?

When tragedy darkens the landscape and the news is full of images of suffering, what do we tell our children? Do we tell them there is no hope, that all is lost? Do we throw up our hands in defeat and give up the good fight?

Americans are a people of steadfast faith. We believe that no matter what terrible thing happens, we will get through it if we come together. We believe in silver linings and that good can come out of the ashes of evil. We struggle and mourn, we grieve and accept. We forgive and go on. We never lose hope in ourselves, our people, our nation.

We will tell our children what we have always told them in times of fear and chaos: With the coming of the dawn is a brand-new day, a new chance to love each other more deeply and to begin to heal. We will hold our children close to us and promise them a future filled with peace and opportunity.

And then we will roll up our collective sleeves and set about fulfilling that promise, because we owe it to each new generation to leave behind us a legacy of good, of prosperity, of potential. We do what needs to be done in our homes, our communities, and our cities to rebuild our nation even stronger than it ever was before.

That is what we tell our children.

A Second Look

Give me eyes, O God, to take a second look at those who think, act, and look different than me. Help me take seriously your image of them. Equip me with acceptance and courage as I hold out a welcoming hand knowing that you are present wherever strangers' hands meet.

. . . he brings us alongside someone else who is going through hard times so that we can be there for that person just as God was there for us.

2 Corinthians 1:4, The Message

Appreciating Life

I have survived a disaster, Lord. I am still able to live and love. From this I have learned to appreciate so much more, such as the song of a bird, the smell of a rose, and the grasp of a baby's hand. Thank you for allowing me to live another day and for teaching me about what's really important in life. Amen.

*H*eal my heart today, I pray. I am so lonely. I feel desolate, I really am alone. Oh God, be my companion and helper in the days to come. Have mercy on me, I beg you. In Jesus' precious name. Amen.

Opting for Hope

*G*iven a choice between hope and despair when trouble
hits, Lord, I pick hope. It doesn't trivialize suffering or dismiss
evil; it simply trusts your promise to make all things new again.

*F*aith is a silent declaration of inner wholeness amidst the
outer appearance of chaos and disorder.

*I*f God is for us, who is against us?

Romans 8:31

*W*hile struggles rage, we cling together by candlelight, drawing courage from one another until the dawn comes again. It is then that God will bring us a happier day.

Reflections of Light

*H*eld up to your light, our broken hearts can become prisms that scatter rainbows on the wall. Our pain is useless as it is, God, just as a prism is a useless chunk of glass until light passes through it. Remind us that the smallest ray of sun in a shower can create a rainbow. Use our tears as the showers and your love as the sun. Looking up, we see the tiniest arches of hope in the lightening sky.

*T*hank you, Lord, for holding my hand as I take the next step in my journey forward.

America, The Beautiful

O beautiful for spacious
   skies,
For amber waves of grain,
For purple mountain
   majesties
Above the fruited plain!
America! America!
God shed his grace on thee
And crown thy good
With brotherhood
From sea to shining sea!

O beautiful for pilgrim feet
Whose stern impassioned
   stress
A thoroughfare for freedom
   beat

Across the wilderness!
America! America!
God mend thine every flaw,
Confirm thy soul
In self-control,
Thy liberty in law!

O beautiful for heroes proved
In liberating strife,
Who more than self the
   country loved
And mercy more than life!
America! America!
May God thy gold refine,
Till all success
Be nobleness,
And every gain divine!

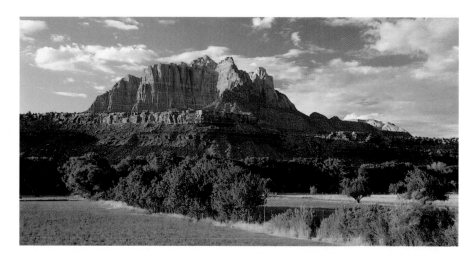

O beautiful for patriot dream
That sees beyond the years
Thine alabaster cities gleam
Undimmed by human tears!
America! America!
God shed his grace on thee
And crown thy good
With brotherhood
From sea to shining sea!

O beautiful for halcyon skies,
For amber waves of grain,
For purple mountain
    majesties
Above the enameled plain!
America! America!
God shed his grace on thee
Till souls wax fair
As earth and air
And music-hearted sea!

O beautiful for pilgrim feet,
Whose stern impassioned
    stress
A thoroughfare for freedom
    beat
Across the wilderness!

America! America!
God shed his grace on thee
Till paths be wrought
Through wilds of thought
By pilgrim foot and knee!

O beautiful for glory-tale
Of liberating strife
When once and twice,
For man's avail
Men lavished precious life!
America! America!
God shed his grace on thee
Till selfish gain
No longer stain
The banner of the free!

O beautiful for patriot dream
That sees beyond the years
Thine alabaster cities gleam
Undimmed by human tears!
America! America!
God shed his grace on thee
Till nobler men
Keep once again
Thy whiter jubilee!

Katharine Lee Bates, 1893

The Lord is my shepherd, I shall not want. He makes me lie down in green pastures; he leads me beside still waters; he restores my soul. He leads me in right paths for his name's sake. Even though I walk through the darkest valley, I fear no evil; for you are with me; your rod and your staff—they comfort me. You prepare a table before me in the presence of my enemies; you anoint my head with oil; my cup overflows. Surely goodness and mercy shall follow me all the days of my life, and I shall dwell in the house of the Lord my whole life long.

Psalm 23

I Pray for Others

Lord, I spend so much time praying for myself that I often forget to pray for the rest of the world. I'd like to spend some time right now praying for my family...my friends and neighbors...pastors...those on mission fields...our schoolteachers...our government and those in power throughout the world...the homeless...the sick...those who are in mourning...the hungry...the hopeless...and the unsaved. Amen.

With malice toward none;
With charity for all;
With firmness in the right,
    as God gives us to see the right,
Let us strive on to finish the work we are in;
To bind up the nation's wounds;
To care for him who shall have borne the battle
And for his widow,
And his orphan—
To do all which may achieve and cherish a just and lasting
    peace among ourselves,
And with all nations.

Abraham Lincoln

Hope and patience
are two sovereign
remedies for all, the
surest reposals, the
softest cushions to
lean on in adversity.

Robert Burton

Bless Our Leaders

Almighty God, bless this country and those whom you have chosen to lead it. So often we fear for the future of this land we love. We see the scars of violence and the heartbreak of those who are left in its wake. We see corruption, and we pray for your forgiveness. Please bless us all with your wisdom and discernment, God. Turn the hearts of this country back to you so that we might become all you intended for us to be . . . beacons of light in the world you created.

I only regret that I have but one life to lose for my country.

The last words of American patriot Nathan Hale
before he was executed by the British in 1776

A despairing heart mumbles, "God is doing nothing." A hopeful heart inquires, "God, what are you going to do next?" and looks forward to celebrating God's awesome ingenuity.

Small Signs of Hope

*W*hen trouble strikes, O God, we are restored by small signs of hope found in ordinary places. We receive random acts of kindness from friends, and sometimes even strangers, who share our pain and offer us support. Help us collect these acts as if they were mustard seeds that can grow into a spreading harvest of well-being.

I awoke this morning with devout thanksgiving for my friends, the old and the new.

Ralph Waldo Emerson (1803–1882)

*D*on't worry about anything; instead, pray about everything; tell God your needs and don't forget to thank him for the answers. If you do this you will experience God's peace, which is far more wonderful than the human mind can understand. His peace will keep your thoughts and your hearts quiet and at rest as you trust in Christ Jesus.

Philippians 4:6–7 TLB

Lighting My Way

I feel healing rising up like the morning sun, breaking and broadening slowly on the horizon of my heart. It comes after a long darkness, God, but I realize now that even in the night-

time of my pain, you were with me, sending your comfort and care like the moon and the stars, keeping watch over my life.

Thank you for lighting my way through the night and bringing the blessing of dawn again.

I will not leave you comfortless: I will come to you.

John 14:18 KJV

Beneath the Stars and Stripes

*L*ook closely, very closely, at an American flag and you will see that just beneath the bold stripes and bright stars is a tapestry quilt comprised of tens of millions of tiny squares. Each square represents a unique citizen of this great nation, and no two squares are exactly alike.

Examine the diversity, the variety of the squares. There is the friendly New Jersey Italian grocer ready to give you the shirt off his back, and the lovely Irish mother of three in Utah who bakes a delicious chocolate cake. There is the  Egyptian doctor in Oregon who often serves the poor in his community for free, and the Cuban boy in Florida who loves baseball as much as life itself. Can you see the little Chinese girl learning how to swim in a New York public pool?

The diversity of a nation we call our homeland is represented in the very fabric that makes up our flag, a fabric so strong that nothing can tear it apart.

The Lord is good, a stronghold in a day of trouble; he protects those who take refuge in him.

Nahum 1:7

Wait on the Lord: be of good courage, and he shall strengthen thine heart.

Psalm 27:14 KJV

Faith is leaning on the only one who is able to hold me up.

Cups Running Over With Anger

God of peace, what are we to do with our anger? In the wake of trouble, it fills us to overflowing. Sometimes our anger is the only prayer we can bring you. We are relieved and grateful to know that you are sturdy enough to bear all we feel and say.

Where do we go from here? Is there life after fury? What will we be without our anger when it's all that has fueled us?

When we are still, we hear your answer: "Emptied." But then we would be nothing.

Remind us that, in your redeeming hands, "nothing" can become of great use, as a gourd hollowed out becomes a cup or a bowl only when emptied.

When the time comes for us to empty ourselves of this abundance of anger, make us into something useful.

When disaster comes, reminding me of how little control I really have over some things in life, I am humbled and made aware again of how much I need you to be my source of strength and comfort.

And when I mourn the loss of temporal possessions, suddenly lost due to unforeseen circumstances, I give thanks that you are the eternal one who will never leave me nor forsake me. In this assurance, I find an indestructible hope and the courage I need to go on.

Give me liberty, or give me death!

Revolutionary War patriot Patrick Henry

. . . whenever you face trials of any kind, consider it nothing but joy, because you know that the testing of your faith produces endurance; and let endurance have its full effect, so that you may be mature and complete, lacking in nothing.

James 1:2–4

Let Me Help

*H*elp me to see with new eyes today—especially the burden of care that others conceal within themselves. Grant me insight to see beyond smiling faces into hearts that hurt. And when I recognize the pain, Lord, let me reach out.

*R*emind us, Lord, that you dwell among the simplest of people. You are the God of the poor, walking with beggars, making your home with the sick and the helpless. Keep us mindful that no matter how much we have, our great calling is to depend on you for everything, every day of our lives.

*L*ord, I often pray for others when I need to pray with others. Show me the power of shared prayer as I meet with others in your name and in your presence. Amen.

*I*t is you who light my lamp;
the Lord, my God, lights up my
   darkness.
This God—his way is perfect;
the promise of the Lord proves true;
he is a shield for all who take
   refuge in him.

Psalm 18:28, 30

*W*hen the world around us grows cold and chaotic, faith is the balm that soothes a fearful heart and the blanket that comforts an anxious mind.

Lady Liberty

"Give me your tired, your poor, your huddled masses yearning to breathe free." So wrote Emma Lazarus in her poem "The New Colossus" in 1883. Her words are inscribed on the Statue of Liberty, which to this day serves as a symbol of welcoming and acceptance for millions of people longing to be free.

A gift from the French to the Americans, the world-renowned statue, weighing in at 225 tons, was sculpted by Frederic Auguste Bartholdi and presented to President Grover Cleveland in 1886. The statue stands at the entrance to Ellis Island National Park, rising more than 150 feet into the sky. The seven spikes in the crown represent the seven oceans of the world, over which so many millions of immigrants came, and still come, to make America their homeland. Her torch represents "enlightenment." Her 25 windows symbolize the "natural minerals" of the earth, and her toga stands for the Ancient Republic of Rome.

Most people know her only as a symbol of true liberty and freedom. But for those not born on American soil, she is so much more. She is a savior, a hero, a guardian angel, with a torch that shines through the night and fog, offering her "worldwide welcome" to anyone seeking to find the fulfillment of their hopes and dreams upon her abundant shores.

She is Lady Liberty. She is America.

Sanctuary

Source of all life and love, let this nation be a place of goodness and opportunity, a haven for those who are lonely, a sanctuary of peace in the midst of the storm. Above all, let us reflect the kindness of your own heart, day by day.

*L*ord, I want so much for everyone to know you, to turn to you, and to walk with you. Please use me today, in any way you choose, to bring others into your eternal family. In Jesus' precious name, I pray. Amen.

*H*elp me to be always mindful of your presence. Fill me with your peace, grant me your mercy, and lead me in your ways. Amen.

We have a great deal more kindness than is ever spoken.

Ralph Waldo Emerson (1803–1882)

Ay, this is freedom!—these pure skies
Were never stained with village smoke:
The fragrant wind, that through them flies,
  Is breathed from wastes by plough unbroke.
Here, with my rifle and my steed,
  And her who left the world for me,
I plant me, where the red deer feed
  In the green desert—and am free.

Broad are these streams—my steed obeys,
  Plunges, and bears me through the tide.
Wide are these woods—I tread the maze
  Of giant stems, nor ask a guide.
I hunt till day's last glimmer dies.

William Cullen Bryant (1794–1878), from "The Hunter of the Prairies"

The Pledge of Allegiance

I pledge allegiance to the flag of the

United States
of America and
to the Republic
for which it
stands, one
Nation under
God, indivisible,
with liberty and justice for all.

Doves on the Horizon

*T*roubles, dear Lord, have cast us loose from assumptions and certainties, and we are bobbing like rudderless boats on a stormy surf. Though all hope seems gone, we spot doves on

the horizon. Doves in the smile of a neighbor; in the wisdom of a counselor; in good laughs or hearty, cleansing tears; in the flash of hope.

We can see our way through the storm, guided by your love-winged messengers.

*B*lessed are those who mourn, for they will be comforted.

Matthew 5:4

Listen to the Lion

We live our lives never knowing our own capacity for courage, for bravery, for valor and heroism. Then one day we awaken to tragedy. Though our first reaction is shock and fear, as the hours pass something begins to rumble deep inside of us. The sound gets louder as we take action to protect ourselves, our families, our communities.

Suddenly, the noise becomes deafening, rising up over the entire nation as one person and another and another discovers the courage of a lion residing within them. One by one we set that lion free to move with boldness and certainty, with compassion and fierce protectiveness, toward the challenges placed before us.

We listen to the lion inside each of us, and we let it roar.

Hope comes as a ray of sun amidst the cold, dark rain, moving us into the light, where love can heal our pain.

For Everyone in Times of Trouble

O Lord, hear my prayer for all who are in trouble this day.
Comfort those who are facing the loss of a loved one.
Encourage those who are finding it difficult to believe in the
 future.
Heal those who are suffering.
Uphold those who are being tempted in any way today.
In all these things, I ask your blessing. Amen.

*L*ord, bring your calm to my anxious thoughts; bring your
peace to the turmoil. Let this be a starting point for our grow-
ing trust in your goodness. Amen.

We have seen the state of our Union in the endurance of rescuers, working past exhaustion. We have seen the unfurling of flags, the lighting of candles, the giving of blood, the saying of prayers—in English, Hebrew, and Arabic. We have seen the decency of a loving and giving people, who have made the grief of strangers their own. My fellow citizens, for the last nine days, the entire world has seen for itself the state of our Union—and it is strong.

President George W. Bush, from his televised
address to Congress, September 20, 2001

Suffering produces endurance, and endurance produces character, and character produces hope.

Romans 5:3–4

Help Me Believe

*D*ear God, help my unbelief.

When I'm in pain, I forget that you care about me.

I forget that you have helped me through other trials.

I forget that you hold me in your arms to keep me safe.

I forget that you feel the pain I feel.

I forget that you love me.

I forget that I am important to you.

Show me your presence—let me feel your enveloping love.

Heal my hurting soul. Amen.

*I*t is my earnest hope, and indeed the hope of all mankind, that from this solemn occasion a better world shall emerge out of the blood and carnage of the past. A world founded upon faith and understanding, a world dedicated to the dignity of man and the fulfillment of his most cherished wish for freedom, tolerance and justice.... Let us pray that peace be now restored to the world and that God will preserve it always. These proceedings are now closed.

General Douglas MacArthur, accepting the Japanese surrender aboard the U.S.S. Missouri *on September 2, 1945*

Vietnam Veterans Memorial

NE H CRUMPTON • FREDERICK W COOPER
Jr • BILLY H PEEBLES • ROBERT A PRUDEN
LUIS A CRUZ • RAYMO...
MARTINEZ SOTO • CHAR...
R• PETER J LANDR... • ROBERT K HOFFMAN
GORDON B SEARS • NICHOLA...
ID HERNANDE... RODRIGUE...
ONAL... SOLE... CHARLES V DONOHUE
...NHIL... MINIO C... YTENO
D FISHER • CHRISTOPHER W... RGENS
...LU... SHEP... WILLIAM...
IS A REX... RAZIE... ONALD E GERSTNER
M DEWALT • WALDEMAR S GRZ...
CURTIS RICHARD...
... DANIEL J JES...
...OLE...DD...SON • JOSE G BAR...
...REDDIE DACUS • TITUS...
...ER • JOE BILLY M...
...ELSKA • WILLIAM L AIKE...
...SWORT... Jr • ROBERT H GU...
...T • JOHN G STR...
...ARD P ALLEN • PAUL J CO...
...CHA • FRANK R HITES...
...JAMES M... MAN • PERRY A MITCHE...
ZAMUDIO J... ARENCE R PRITCHAR...
...ROSS... RICHARD W AT...OD
...ERT G DRAPE... BRUCE L HANKINS
...BAS • JAMES F RILEY • JOHN...
KENNETH D...ONS • JOSEPH C...LEE
RUSSELL G DAN... RICHARD...
...A DONNEL... CLEVELAND...
RANDALL P MANELA • BENTO...
...N • JAMES E STOLZ Jr • ROBERT...
THOMAS R BIERLINE • JOHN R GRISAR...
...MAS L OSTEEN Jr • WILLIAM J PERRYMAN
Jr• FRANKLIN R AKANA • PHILLIP J BARBA
WILLIAM E FLEMING Jr • THEODORE ISOM
OYLE • ROBERT L SHRINER • RAY E TANNER
HOMAS E BRADLEY • CURTERS J BURNETT
RG • TOMMY BOWENS • JEFFREY A COFFIN
EZ • ROBERT D KAVICH • MARK A LARSON
DOUGLASS T WHELESS • DANIEL J CHAVEZ
AIR • VERNON G ZORNES • IAN McINTOSH
R • JAMES E ESKRIDGE • NORMAN F EVANS
RREN H MOBLEY • BENJAMIN J ANTHONY
O • WILLARD G STORIE • FRANK D TINSLEY
ART • LAWRENCE E SCOTT • LYLE D HAYES
ELL • DAVID E KILLIAN • PHILIP E RICHARD
ALLEN J BODIN • RAMON A HERNANDEZ
T• FREDERICK R NEEF • WILLIAM B O'KIEFF
JI • CHARLES F CREAMER III • GARY E FIELD
Y • JAMES B POWELL Jr • EUGENE PRINCE Jr
LLIAMS • GARY ANDERSON • JOHN R BEAN
FRANKLIN D DEFENBAUGH • JACK R GIBBS
RONALD R GREENHOUSE • RALPH S GUCK
ERT B JOHNSON • WILLIAM D KENNEDY III
ERG • LEE ROY E LINTON • SAMMIE J LONG
UGLAS H PARRIS • NORBERT A PODHAJSKY
NEIDER • BOBBY D SEAY • DONALD A SLATE
ORF • HARRY A WATSON • JAMES B YOUNG
DOUGLAS S BRIDGERS • CHARLES R COILEY
DS • ROBERT S GEER • DONALD L GOLDEN
BENJAMIN R NELSON Jr • PATRICK J PAULICH
ER W ANDERSON Jr • ROBERT L BLACKWELL
...GL• ERIC L GRIFFITH • JOHN H HOLMES
...STEPHEN C SELLETT

THOMAS R BRADLEY • RICHARD E TABOR • ROBERT B MICHALK • GERARD CORRIVEAU • MIKE • CARLETON P BALDAUF • RODNEY E MC
RICHARD H SANSBURY • KEITH R W CURRY • WILLIAM C VASEY • RUSSEL C NELSON • ROBERT L CRAIG • GORDON
DENNIS R WATTERSON • JAIME LABOY • ROBERT DEGEN • DOUGLAS M BECKMAN • CHARLES...
CRAIG A SYSAK • BENNIE F JONES • JAMES R SHAW • BILLY W HARTWICK • JAMES H CART...
KENNETH A DAHL • GORDON L WIRTH Jr • DAVID W LILLEY • JOHN E STEWART • PATRIC
PHILIP J ADAMS • STEPHEN P KRUG • DOUGLAS O FORD • WILLARD E WOODY • LOUIS PAYNE Sr • CLINTON C RO
EDWARD W BETHARDS • JOE H LILLIE • CORNELIUS H RAM • JERRY T HICKEY • WILLIAM T
RICHARD L RUSHLOW • JOSE R SANDOVAL • THOMAS F IRVIN • RICHARD V BLACKBURN • JAMES T
DARREL J CLODFELTER • STEPHEN E HENDRICKS • WILLIAM E STRACNER • WILLIAM F JOHNSON • LEE W CLORE • ALLEN
DENNY RAY EASTER • ROBERT J KAPUSTA • EDWARD J KAPUSTA • FRANCIS J THORPE • DAVID J MEYER • LEO
DONALD W SMITH • RUDOLPH C THOMAS • HAROLD E CARR • BILLY RAY PRICE Jr • REX A VOC
DANIEL F COX • JOSEPH W GAA Jr • EDGAR L WEST Sr • JERRY LEE MOFFETT • ROBERT J LA
WILLIAM A MALENFANT • CURTIS W MOORE • JAMES A HARWOOD • BILLY RAY ANDERSON • DAVID
ROBERT E SHARPE • WILLIAM R ZEYEN • WILLIAM NAKI III • GERALD F KINSMAN • DAVID
PAUL DARBY • JOHN E DAVIS • JEFF T BARNETT Sr • DELBERT R PORTER • BRIAN F
HERBERT S HINSON • ROGER G HOLLER • DONALD G DETRICK • CHARLES R BESS • DEWAINE L B
TERRY F MEZERA • EARL NELSON • REINALDO REIN RODRIGUEZ • MARTIN JIM Jr • PAUL E LEARY Jr • CARLTON J
LEE D STUART Jr • CHARLES D StCLAIR • ROY RODRIGUEZ SALINAS • BRUCE C
WILLIAM B BLACKMON Jr • ALBERT L BROWN • WILLIAM H THIGPEN • JOHNNY N WARD Jr • JOHN
JOHN H GEDDINGS • MALCOLM J LYONS • DAVID W COON • JOHN L DOBROSKI • DANIEL K ER
PERRY M SMITH • CECIL W SOUTHERLAND • ROBERT H MIRRER • JESSE E NIXON • JAMES N
JOSHUA M DANIELS • EUGENE T GILMORE • JOSEPH S TIDWELL • WILLIAM F AARONSON IV • RON
GLENN R ETHINGTON • JESUS A GONZALES • STEPHEN A ALTSCHAFFL • LARRY J PRICE • WILBUR
JAMES F THAMES • HESSIE A BROOKS • RONALD D ROWSEY • WILLI
ARTHUR S NABBEN • RONALD D STEPHENSON • JAMES R GARTEN • TOMMY H IVEY • ROBERT P
GREGORY S KARGER • EUGENE J LEVICKIS • STEVEN W MOLL • RONALD M GARRISON • ROBERT
RONNIE G VAUGHAN • LARRY D BEAN • BARTOW W POTTS Jr • SAMUEL
HUGH D OPPERMAN • GREGORY L PEFFER • MICHAEL H PETTY • DENNIS R SCHOSSOW • KENNETH
DONALD L SENTI • FREDERICK A VIGIL • ALFONSO A BRITO • WILLIAM H
RONALD J REVIS • JAMES L COLWE • STEPHEN L LINDSAY • CALVIN E MILAM • GEORG
RICHARD C PORTER • MERRELL E BRUMLEY Jr • WILLIAM O CREECH Jr • JUAN E GONZALES • WILLIAM
JAMES P MARKEY Jr • WILLIAM D NICODEMUS • GEORGE L ROBERTSON • ROBERTO L CANAS • JO
DEWIGHT E NORTON • STEVEN J OLCOTT • WILLIAM F REICHERT • JAMES E WEATHERSBY • GARNEY E
DEAN A HARRIS • RONALD M RIGDON • ARTHUR A SMITH • MICHAEL E WILLIAMS • HAROLD B
DAVID I MIXTER • ROBERT L PULLIAM • JEFFREY L BARLOW • HAROLD E BIRKY • JAMES
ALLEN C ELL • RAFAEL GARCIA PAGAN • RONALD W HACKNEY • RONALD N JASINSKI
JOHN R MILLER • ROBERT A SISK • JOHNNY C SPEARS • JOHNNY E TIVIS • PATRICK G CARTWRIGHT • LA
JOSEPH W CASINO • CLYDE W C...LE • GORDON L CRAWFORD • JAMES C HARRIS • LORE
KEITH EN JACKSON • WALTER X AR...OLD • THOMAS C MILLER • STEPHEN A MOORE • STEP
RICHARD D RANDOLPH • KEITH A GODDARD • MICHAEL P AUSTIN • DARRELL W COWAN • ROB
FRANK S McCUTCHEON III • FLOYD RICHARDSON Jr • JOHN C STRA...KY • PHILIP R
LUTHER N BAGNAL III • MARTIN J BURNS • MILDRED R GREEN • LENNART G LANGHORNE • THOMA
ROBERT L STANDERWICK Sr • JOSEPH L STONE • WALLY L EBB • TERENCE W WELDON • ROBER
JACKIE LEE DENNY • SAMUEL H EBERHART • GREG... SOMERS • LARRY H MARSHALL • DAN
ANDRES LOPEZ RAMON • NELSON G RICHARDSON • ...VE R...LL • STEPHEN M TRAYNOR • PATRI
CLIFTON E CALLAHAN • DAVID C JOHNSON • ...COMB • JAMES L PAUL • JOH
...ALEXANDER • KENNETH W
CARL M WOOD • LARRY A WOODBURN • RICHARD A... • MICHAEL J KERL • CA
FRANK J GASPERICH Jr • AMBERS A HAMILTON • WILLIAMS • THEOD
WILLIAM B RHODES • ROBERT J ROGERS • JOSEPH A... • WILLIAM A LARGENT
BRIAN R FOLEY • THOMAS P B KING • RICH... OCHA • DOUGLAS
RUSSELL G BLOCHER • DONALD L MEEHAN Jr • CHARLES... SPOON • HARRY
LEWIS R YATES • ROLAND D TROYANO • BRUCE A VAN... LEY • BAR
THOMAS A SONY • RAFAEL RIVERA BENITEZ • CHA... ROE
LONALD R COLEMAN • THOMAS P DOOD...
KYLE C HOLFELTZ • RANDALL L HARRIS • KEVIN P KNIGH...
LENOX L RATCLIFF • JOHN E ROBERTSON • CHARLES F...
GERALD J TWOREK • GREG R CARTER • BRUC...
MELVIN J FELTON • EDMOND S BLACKBURN Jr • EDGAR...
FRED D PAKELE • NORMAN J PEARSON • PHILLIP J SAND...
MICHAEL C LAWSON • JAMES F COLLINS • DONALD A...
MARK J ROBERTSON • MONETTE V WHITE • JOSEPH R...
OLAN D COLEMAN • JAMES F CONNOR Jr • CHAR...
CLYDE W HANSON • ROY L HELBERT • WAYNE O PATTERSO...
RICHARD W OKEEFE • WILLIAM L WILLIAMS • JOS...
WILLIS G UHLS • WILLIAM J JOHNSON • ...
WILLIE GARDNER • JAMES V PICARAZZI • JAMES...
ARTHUR E McLEOD • JOSEPH V MARTIN • ...
MICHAEL D ADKINS • STEVEN L SEIGLER • FREDERIC...
KARLHEINZ S SEIBERLING • JAMES R JESKE • PERRY W...
DOUGLAS L HORN • JAMES R BROS...
...IVAN R ASPER Jr • JAMES R B...

Why, O Lord, do you stand far off? Why do you hide yourself in times of trouble?

David, Psalm 10:1 NIV

In the midst of mourning life's troubles, you come to us. In the darkness, your spirit moves, spreading light like a shower of stars against a stromy night sky.

The Marines' Hymn

*F*rom the Halls of Mon-
   tezuma
To the shores of Tripoli
We fight our country's battles
On the land as on the sea.
First to fight for right and
   freedom
And to keep our honor clean;
We are proud to claim the
   title
Of United States Marines.

Our flag's unfurled to every
   breeze
From dawn to setting sun;
We have fought in every
   clime and place
Where we could take a gun.
In the snow of far-off North-
   ern lands
And in sunny tropic scenes;
You will find us always on the
   job—
The United States Marines.

Here's health to you and to
   our Corps

Which we are proud to serve;
In many a strife we've fought
   for life
And never lost our nerve.
If the Army and the Navy
Ever look on Heaven's
   scenes,
They will find the streets are
   guarded
By United States Marines.

Author Unknown (circa 1875)

Carry Me

*L*ord God, today was almost more than I could bear. I am afraid to face tomorrow. How can I know that things will be OK when everything seems so wrong right now? I have no strength left inside to take the next step, so I'm asking you to pick me up and carry me. I know you offer your grace as a gift of sufficiency, providing me with everything I need to go on. I accept your grace right now. Help me rest in the knowledge that you will be with me, taking me through each moment that lies ahead.

*T*he rain came down, the streams rose, and the winds blew and beat against that house; yet it did not fall, because it had its foundation on the rock.

Matthew 7:25 NIV

*I*t is the duty of all nations to acknowledge the providence of Almighty God, to obey His will, to be grateful for His benefits, and humbly implore His protection and favor.

George Washington

*T*wo are better than one. . . . For if they fall, one will lift up the other.

Ecclesiastes 4:9–10

*T*hese are the times that try men's souls. The summer soldier and the sunshine patriot will, in this crisis, shrink from the service of their country; but he that stands it now, deserves the love and thanks of man and woman. Tyranny, like hell, is not easily conquered; yet we have this consolation with us, that the harder the conflict, the more glorious the triumph. What we obtain too cheap, we esteem too lightly: It is dearness only that gives every thing its value. Heaven knows how to put a proper price upon its goods; and it would be strange indeed if so celestial an article as Freedom should not be highly rated.

Thomas Payne, 1776

*F*or surely I know the plans I have for you, says the Lord, plans for your welfare and not for harm, to give you a future with hope.

Jeremiah 29:11

Blessed Are Those Who Give

*B*lessed are those who give their lives for what they believe, for they will one day receive glory with God in heaven.

Blessed are those who grieve and mourn, for they will one day know a joy beyond earthly measure.

Blessed are those who dare to rebuild from the ashes of disaster, for they will one day see their visions manifested.

Blessed are those who risk their lives to help another, for they will one day be exalted as angels.

Blessed are those who keep order amidst chaos, for they will one day know a peace that passes all understanding.

Blessed are those who pray for their fellow citizens, for they will one day find their own prayers answered.

Blessed are those who donate their time, money, and life blood to save others, for they will one day be rewarded with the bounty of the heavens.

And blessed are those who keep love alive even in the midst of hatred and fear, for they will one day know the greatest love of all in the arms of God.

Weeping may linger for the night, but joy comes with the morning.

Psalm 30:5

Today I long to make a difference—to pass along peace and joy and somehow resurrect hope in weary hearts.

We, therefore, the representatives of the United States of America, in general congress assembled, appealing to the Supreme Judge of the world for the rectitude of our intentions, do, in the name and by authority of the good people of these colonies, solemnly publish and declare, that these united colonies are, and of right ought to be, free and independent states; that they are absolved from all allegiance to the British Crown, and that all political connection between them and the state of Great Britain is, and ought to be, totally dissolved; and that as free and independent states they have full power to levy war, conclude peace, contract alliances, establish commerce, and to do all other acts and things which independent states may of right do. And for the support of this declaration, with a firm reliance on the protection of Divine Providence, we mutually pledge to each other our lives, our fortunes, and our sacred honor.

From the Declaration of Independence, composed in 1775 by Thomas Jefferson, John Adams, Benjamin Franklin, Roger Sherman, and Robert R. Livingston

Blessed are those who trust in the Lord.

Jeremiah 17:7

Sharing

We are blessed to live in a country so full of riches, Lord, that we take most of them for granted. Yet we know there are places in the world where children must go to bed hungry, and their mothers cry late into the night because they don't know what tomorrow will bring. Thank you for blessing us with your abundance, Lord. May we have hearts to share what we have with others, and may we never cease to praise you for all you have given to us. Amen.

Faith makes the discords of the present the harmonies of the future.

Robert Collyer

*I*n God We Trust.

*Imprinted on American
currency since 1864*

*L*ove is patient,
love is kind. It does
not envy, it does
not boast, it is not
proud. It is not
rude, it is not self-
seeking, it is not
easily angered, it
keeps no record of
wrongs. Love does
not delight in evil
but rejoices with
the truth. It always protects, always trusts, always hopes,
always perseveres. Love never fails.

1 Corinthians 13:4–8 NIV

Bringing Out the Best in Us

*I*t is no coincidence that TV shows of true-life survivors are popular among American viewers. Americans know what it takes and what it means to survive, and to thrive. For we have displayed over and over the ability to rise to the occasion during times of distress.

Whether it is a hurricane, earthquake, school shooting, or act of terrorism, people respond with courage, compassion, and concern. Families find their way home to each other. Tragedies are shared by entire communities, disasters bring together citizens of neighboring states, and devastating violence unites a nation. When things go bad, the good in Americans rings out clear and true. When the worst occurs, it brings out the best in us. We display resilience and fortitude we never knew we had.

Americans are not victims. We are healers, helpers, and teachers—shining examples for the rest of the world. We are friends for other nations to lean on. We are guiding lights for the rest of the world to follow.

We are survivors.

The difference between a person who quits and one who keeps on through storm and struggle is a hopeful heart.

He will wipe away all tears from their eyes, and there shall be no more death, nor sorrow, nor crying, nor pain.

All of that has gone forever.

Revelation 21:4 TLB

Let Me Be a Healer

I wish to extend my love to the world, Lord.

So give me hands quick enough to work on behalf of the weak.

Cause my feet to move swiftly in aid of the needy.

Let my mouth speak words of encouragement and new life.

And give my heart an ever-deepening joy through it all.

*O*h God, bring your cool caress to those who are suffering. By your spirit, lift the spirits of the soldiers, giving comfort to those who are afraid. Strengthen them and give them renewed energy for their tasks. Amen.

Letting Go

Sometimes, God, I wish I could control the events in my life that cause me anxiety. Please help me to let go of my need to control things and to allow your plan for my life to unfold before me. I will trust in you, God, to show me the way.

This nation has placed its destiny in the hands and heads and hearts of its millions of free men and women; and its faith in freedom under the guidance of God. Freedom means the supremacy of human rights everywhere. Our support goes to those who struggle to gain those rights or keep them. Our strength is our unity of purpose.

To that high concept there can be no end save victory.

Franklin Delano Roosevelt, from his 1941 message to Congress

God gives burdens, also shoulders.

Yiddish proverb

My Country 'Tis of Thee

*M*y country, 'tis of thee,
Sweet land of liberty,
    Of thee I sing;
Land where my fathers died,
Land of the Pilgrims' pride,
From every mountain-side
    Let Freedom ring.

My native country, thee,
Land of the noble free—
    Thy name I love;
I love thy rocks and rills,
Thy woods and templed hills:
My heart with rapture thrills
    Like that above.

Let music swell the breeze,
And ring from all the trees
    Sweet Freedom's song;
Let mortal tongues awake,
Let all that breathe partake,
Let rocks their silence
break—
    The sound prolong.

Our fathers' God, to Thee,
Author of liberty,
    To thee we sing;
Long may our land be bright
With Freedom's holy light;
Protect us by Thy might,
    Great God, our King.

Baptist clergyman and poet Samuel
Francis Smith (1808–1895)

*B*y day the Lord commands his steadfast love, and at night his song is with me.

Psalm 42:8

We pray but don't feel answered, Lord. Help us understand that regardless of the answers we want, being connected to you through prayer is changing us into "can do" people. We *can* find solutions, we *can* try again. Looking back, we understand you did answer.

The name of American, which belongs to you in your national capacity, must always exalt the just pride of patriotism more than any appellation derived from local discriminations. With slight shades of difference, you have the same religion, manners, habits, and political principles. You have in a common cause fought and triumphed together. The independence and liberty you possess are the work of joint councils and joint efforts, of common dangers, sufferings, and successes.

George Washington, from his farewell address in 1796

Only You, O Lord

*L*ord, when our throats are dry, shower us with the nourishing rain of your love. When our stomachs cry out in hunger, feed us with the satisfying manna of your presence. When our bodies are tired from fighting the forces of evil, comfort us in the shelter of your loving arms.

When our minds reel with confusion, shine the light of clarity and wisdom into the dark corners, dispelling the shadows that bind us. When our souls tremble in fear, soothe us with your healing balm of inner peace. When our spirits are low and discouraged, charge us with the fire of your passion for righteousness.

We are open channels, and only you, O Lord, can fill our needs.

*Y*ou who have made me see many troubles and calamities will revive me again; from the depths of the earth you will bring me up again. You will increase my honor, and comfort me once again.

Psalm 71:20–21

Grains of Sand

*W*e are surprised by joy, God of creation, when we see despair outwitted by simple acts of love. Keep us searching, believing, and loving those who are in need.

I'm not feeling very safe in my own home these days, God. I pray that you would place a hedge of safety around this dwelling and prevent all evil from crossing over. Keep us safe, and help us to accept your protection. Amen.

*I*n all human sorrows nothing gives comfort but love and faith.

Leo Tolstoy, Anna Karenina

*H*ope is the glue that binds the pieces of a shattered dream, making it shiny and new and whole again.

Pointing Fingers

*W*hen life goes awry, Lord, and I need someone to blame, I point a finger at you. Heaven help me, I want it both ways: you as the sender as well as the fixer of trouble. Help me to understand that you don't will trouble, for what could you possibly gain? And when the good you want for me isn't possible in the randomness of life, remind me that you are with me.

Empower Us

My Creator, blessed is your presence. For you and you alone give me power to walk through dark valleys into the light again. You and you alone give me hope when there seems no end to my suffering. You and you alone give me peace when the noise of my life overwhelms me. I ask that you give this same power, hope, and peace to all who know discouragement, that they, too, may be emboldened and renewed by your everlasting love. Amen.

In this unconquerably and justifiably optimistic nation nothing undertaken by free men and free women is impossible.

Playwright Robert E. Sherwood (1896–1955)

Do not let your hearts be troubled. Believe in God, believe also in me. . . . Peace I leave with you; my peace I give to you. I do not give to you as the world gives. Do not let your hearts be troubled, and do not let them be afraid.

John 14:1

A wise mind knows that adverse events are blessed opportunities for growth in disguise.

*L*et us resolve that we the people will build an American opportunity society in which all of us—white and black, rich and poor, young and old—will go forward together arm in arm. Again, let us remember that though our heritage is one of bloodlines from every corner of the Earth, we are all Americans pledged to carry on this last, best hope of man on Earth.

Ronald Reagan, from his 1985 inaugural address

There is no potion so powerful, no pill so amazing, no promised reward so alluring as the certain belief that something good can happen tomorrow.

I will study the way that is blameless. When shall I attain it? I will walk with integrity of heart within my house.

Psalm 101:2

Bless Our Heroes

We come to you today, Lord, to ask you to bless all those who go out of their way to help others. In particular, we ask your blessing on the firefighters and police officers who risk their lives each and every day. But we also ask you to bless the doctors, nurses, pastors, and people in every neighborhood who volunteer to make life a little easier for someone else. Smile down upon all those who reach out to others, Lord. In your name we pray. Amen.

Rejoice in hope, be patient in suffering, persevere in prayer.

Romans 12:12

*T*each us to know, God, that it is at the point of our deepest despair that you are closest. For at those times we can finally admit we have wandered in the dark, without a clue. Yet you have been there with us all along. Thank you for your presence.

*H*umble yourselves therefore under the mighty hand of God, so that he may exalt you in due time. Cast all your anxiety on him, because he cares for you.

1 Peter 5:6–7

The American's Creed

I believe in the United States of America as a government of the people, by the people, for the people; whose just powers are derived from the consent of the governed; a democracy in a republic; a sovereign nation of many sovereign states; a perfect union, one and inseparable; established upon those principles of freedom, equality, justice, and humanity for which American patriots sacrificed their lives and fortunes. I therefore believe it is my duty to my country to love it, to support its constitution, to obey its laws, to respect its flag, and to defend it against all enemies.

William Tyler Page, accepted by
the House of Representatives on April 3, 1918

The liberties of our country, the freedom of our civil constitution, are worth defending at all hazards; and it is our duty to defend them against all attacks.

Samuel Adams
(1722–1803)

Bless us as we weather this conflict. Teach us to love. Simply love.

We Place Our Hope in You

*L*ord, when we have nothing left to hold on to, you provide us with hope as an anchor for our souls. We need that hope now, and we pray that you will fill every broken place in our hearts with its reassuring light. Thank you, Lord, for in you we have an unending supply of hope in the midst of uncertainty and failure. We know that if we could see this situation through your eyes, we would see how you will bring us through it.

We place our hope in you and you only.

Amen.

*H*ope is about believing with a humble heart that tomorrow can be different. It's about knowing that light will come to chase away this darkness.

*T*he best thing about the future is that it only comes one day at a time.

Abraham Lincoln

I will never leave you or forsake you.

Hebrews 13:5

We dare not forget today that we are the heirs of that first revolution. Let the word go forth from this time and place, to friend and foe alike, that the torch has been passed to a new

generation of Americans—born in this century, tempered by war, disciplined by a hard and bitter peace, proud of our ancient heritage— and unwilling to witness or permit the slow undoing of those human rights to which this Nation has always been committed, and to which we are committed today at home and around the world.

Let every nation know, whether it wishes us well or ill, that we shall pay any price, bear any burden, meet any hardship, support any friend, oppose any foe, in order to assure the survival and the success of liberty.

This much we pledge—and more.

John F. Kennedy, from his inaugural address on January 20, 1961

Give Me the Faith

*L*ord, give me the faith to take the next step, even when I don't know what lies ahead. Give me the assurance that even if I stumble and fall, you'll pick me up and put me back on the path. And give me the confidence that, even if I lose faith, you will never lose me. Amen.

*W*hen the earth and all its people quake, it is I who hold its pillars firm.

Psalm 75:3 NIV

*V*ery truly, I tell you, you will weep and mourn, but the world will rejoice; you will have pain, but your pain will turn to joy.

John 16:20

*F*aith, as sturdy as the stone foundation beneath a century-old house, forms the bedrock upon which I stand, unswayed despite the winds of change.

In God We Trust

*G*od, we look to you in times of pain and sorrow for the strength and courage to carry on. We place our lives in your hands as we unite in spirit to lift our nation up on wings of eagles. Bless us this day and every day with your love, that we might then go forth and love one another more fully.

*T*each us your patience and your forgiveness. Show us how to be more tolerant of others, more accepting of their differences, for it is these differences that make our nation so unique. We put our trust in you, dear God, that you will keep watch over us as a loving father keeps watch over his children.

Amen.

*A*s a mother comforts her child, so I will comfort you.

Isaiah 66:13

T here never was night that had no morn.

Dinah Mulock Craik

Overwhelmed

D efeat has stopped me in my tracks. I see no options, no possibilities. Yet paralyzing doubt can be relieved by finding something to believe in, something as simple as blossoms, rainbows, dawn, or a gentle rain. God will find me there.

Come to me, all you that are weary and are carrying heavy burdens, and I will give you rest. Take my yoke upon you, and learn from me; for I am gentle and humble in heart, and you will find rest for your souls. For my yoke is easy, and my burden is light.

Matthew 11:28–30

Because of what America is and what America has done, a firmer courage, a higher hope, inspires the heart of all humanity.

Calvin Coolidge (1872–1933)

A Sign

*T*o those scanning a night sky, you sent a star. To those tending sheep on a silent hill, you sent a voice. What sign, Lord, are you sending me so I can be and do all you intend? Let me hear, see, and accept it when you do.

I will say of the Lord, "He is my refuge and my fortress, my God; in whom I trust."

Psalm 91:2 NIV

The Gift of Faith

No greater gift has God given us than the gift of faith; that deep and steadfast inner knowing that no matter what happens to us, we can call upon the help of a higher power to see us through.

Were it not for our faith, we would not dare to dream the dreams we reach and strive for. Were it not for our faith, we would give up too soon, back down too quickly, and walk away too abruptly from the challenges and obstacles that appear in our paths. Were it not for our faith, we would abandon those who need us when times get tough. Were it not for our faith, we would turn our backs on our own neighbors when disaster or tragedy strikes.

Faith is the invisible glue that binds us together, that holds us fast to our visions of what our lives can be. Without faith, we are weak, frightened creatures hiding our heads in the sand. Without faith, we would never have become the free and powerful people that we are. Without faith, we would never have dared to build machines that fly, send a man to the moon, and cure deadly diseases.

But with faith we can do anything, be anything. We can climb the highest mountain and touch the stars. We can fall and get up and fall and get up again, never surrendering, never giving in. With faith, we are warriors of the heart and spirit, bold and brave and true.

Contributing Writer: Marie D. Jones